This play was produced by Sherman Cymru and first performed at
Sherman Cymru, Cardiff on Wednesday 18 April 2012.

Gwyneth Lewis asserts her moral right to be identified as the author of
this work.

Cover image: Grace Vane Percy
Design: Rhys Huws
Typeset in Wales by Eira Fenn Gaunt
Printed in Wales by Cambrian Printers, Aberystwyth.

ISBN 978-1-907707-06-3

Sherman C   ivestment of
the Arts Co

CAST

Rhian Blythe
Matthew Bulgo
Jaye Griffiths
Nia Gwynne
Kezrena James
Nick Moss
Adam Redmore
Jonah Russell
Eiry Thomas

PRODUCTION TEAM

Director: Amy Hodge
Designer: takis
Lighting Designer: Lee Curran
Composer & Sound Designer: Simon Thorne
Choreographer: Dr. Johan Stjernholm
Assistant Designer: Sara Polonghini
Assistant Director: Peter Scott
Casting: Louis Hammond and Kate Perridge
Company Stage Manager: Brenda Knight
Deputy Stage Manager: Jo Ashberry
Assistant Stage Manager: Charlotte Neville
Deputy Electrician (Sound): Lewis Evans
Construction Manager: Mathew Thomas
Wardrobe Assistant: Angharad Griffin
Design Assistant: Liz Rose
Arial Harness Consultation: James Doyle-Roberts & John Kirk (Citrus Arts)

THANKS

Sherman Cymru gratefully acknowledges Clwyd Theatr Cymru as original co-commissioners of *Clytemnestra*.

SHERMAN CYMRU

We aim to make and present great theatre that is ambitious, inventive and memorable for our audiences, and to create strong, responsive and enriching relationships with our communities. We produce work in both English and Welsh, and tour widely within Wales and the UK.

For more information about Sherman Cymru events visit -
www.shermancymru.co.uk

Calon
Joining Calon will bring you into the heart of Sherman Cymru as you will be contributing to the vital lifeline that the company needs to continue creating great artistic work for all.

Your support will help Sherman Cymru to:
- Produce exceptional work in Welsh and English
- Present productions by the UK's most prestigious companies
- Offer creative opportunities for young people in Cardiff and the surrounding areas
- Develop the talent of many artists and writers
- Work with the many communities of Cardiff, engaging people in the arts.

Calon also gives you benefits that will bring you closer to Sherman Cymru:
- Advance notice of the season's performances and activities
- Seasonal priority booking
- Your name on the Sherman Cymru website
- 10% discount on post-show drinks at the bar

For an annual donation of just £30 (£50 for a couple), you will be making a big difference to Sherman Cymru, both for today and tomorrow.
For further information please contact Emma Goad, Head of Development on 029 2064 6975.

RHIAN BLYTHE
Electra

Theatre

Romeo a Juliet, Plas Drycin, Hen Rebel, Dominos (Theatr Genedlaethol Cymru); *Bitsh* (Cwmni'r Frân Wen); *Porth y Byddar* (Theatr Genedlaethol Cymru/Clwyd Theatr Cymru); *Deep Cut* (Sherman Cymru); *Mae Gynno Ni Hawl Ar Y Ser* (Llwyfan Gogledd Cymru); *Blink* (F.A.B. Theatre); *Unprotected, Never Fear Love* (Velvet Ensemble); *On Emotion* (On Theatre/Soho Theatre); *To Kill a Mockingbird* (Clwyd Theatr Cymru).

Television

Mostyn Fflint 'n Aye, Talcen Caled, Gwaith / Cartref, Man Del, Pen Talar, Blodau (S4C).

Radio

Fire of the Dragon (BBC Radio 4).

Rhian won the Best Actress award at the Edinburgh Festival for her portrayal of Jonesy in Sherman Cymru's *Deep Cut*.

MATTHEW BULGO
Chorus 3 / Watchman

Theatre
A Christmas Carol, The City, The Push and The Pull (Sherman Cymru); *Under Milk Wood* (Royal & Derngate); *My Father's Hands* (Paines Plough); *Hamlet* (Natural Perspectives); *The Exquisite Corpse* (True/Fiction, Wales Millennium Centre and Edinburgh Fringe); *Riddance, BASH* and *Mr. Theatre Comes Home Different* (True/Fiction); *The Ceremony* (Soho Theatre); *The Secret of Belonging, Stella Time, Crazy Gary's Mobile Disco, Gull* (Antic Corporation); *Repeat* (Dirty Protest); *BANK* and *Playing Hamlet* (Kings Head Theatre); *Bloody Sunday* (Tricycle Theatre); *Much Ado About Nothing, Dangerous Liaisons* (Mappa Mundi); *Nowhere: Now Here* (National Theatre Wales).

Film
Colin (Nowhere Fast Productions); *The Architect, Thicker Than Water* (Karakucha Productions).

Writing
Come To Where I'm From (Paines Plough); *Lacuna* (Egin:SpringBoard Sherman Cymru); *Opus* (LOST Theatre); *A Love Story* (Southwark Playhouse); *This Restless Heart* (Velvet Ensemble). Matthew is currently under commission from the London site-specific company, The Squat Collective.

JAYE GRIFFITHS
Clytemnestra

Theatre
*A Woman of No Importance,
Gasping* (Haymarket Theatre);
Salome (Headlong Theatre);
Category B, Seize The Day, Emma
(Tricycle Theatre); *Othello* (Cheek By
Jowl); *A Midsummer Night's Dream*
(Bristol Old Vic); *Julius Caesar*
(Young Vic Theatre); *Wit* (Vaudeville
Theatre).

Television
*Coronation Street, A Touch of Frost,
Hunger, Kingdom* (ITV); *Sherlock,
Criminal Justice, Silent Witness,
Doctors, Rocket Man, Holby City,
The Deputy, Care* (BBC Television);
Skins (E4); *The Bill* (Thames
Television); *Always and Everyone*
(Granada Television); *Wyrd Sister*
(Galafilm); *Bugs* (Carnival Films).

Jaye won the Clarence Derwent
Award for Emilia in *Othello*, 2004.

Nia trained at RADA and will be appearing in *Coriolan/us* with National Theatre Wales this summer.

NIA GWYNNE
Fury 1

Theatre
The Dark Philosophers (National Theatre Wales); *Look Back In Anger* (Northern Stage Company); *Lie Of The Land* (Pleasance, Edinburgh); *The Daughter In Law, Dangerous Corner, Billy Liar, Love Me Slender* (New Vic); *The Almond and the Seahorse* (Sherman Cymru); *Absurd Person Singular* (Bolton Octagon); *To Kill A Mockingbird, The Invention of Love* (Salisbury Playhouse); *Mirandolina* (Royal Exchange); *Ghost City* (Sgript Cymru); *Who Goes There?* (Dreamthinkspeak); *Dogmouth* (The Evidence Room); *Two Nice Girls* (TAPS).

Television
Casualty, EastEnders, Stick or Twist, Belonging (BBC Television); *The Syndicate, The Bill* (ITV); *Pam Fi Duw?* (S4C).

Film
Shadow Dancer (BBC Films/ Element Pictures); *Resistance* (Rich Films); *The Organ Grinder's Monkey* (Film4/Warp Films); *Lemmings* (Day For Night Productions).

Theatre in Wales Best Actress award for *Ghost City*. LA Weekly Best Supporting Actress nominee for *Dogmouth*.

KEZRENA JAMES
Cassandra

Kezrena James was born in Cardiff and trained at Guildford School of Acting (GSA).

Theatre
The Faith Machine (The Royal Court); *An Inspector Calls* (Orange Tree Theatre Company).

Television
Pobol y Cwm (S4C); *Tracy Beaker, Doctors, Crash, Casualty* (BBC Television); *Fit For Duty* (Grosvenor TV).

Voice over
Different (Ruthie Thomas).

Theatre

The Resistable Rise of Arturo Ui (Nottingham Playhouse); *Glengarry Glen Ross* (Manchester Library); *Lost Monsters, The Way Home, Urban Legend, The Mayor of Zalamea, Scouse* (Liverpool Everyman); *Having A Ball, Man of the Moment* (Theatre Royal, York); *W.A.T.E.R. Is Water* (Clwyd Theatr Cymru); *Bonded* (Sheffield Crucible); *End of Season* (Red Ladder).

Television

Birdsong (Working Title TV); *Shameless* (Kudos); *I Shouldn't Be Alive* (Darlow Smithson); *The Accused* (RSJ Films); *Doctors, Casualty, Cops, City Central, EastEnders, Paradise Heights, Merseybeat* (BBC Television); *Coronation Street, The Street, Hillsborough, Police 2020, Always & Everyone* (Granada); *Collision* (Greenlit); *The Bill, Smack the Pony* (Talkback Thames); *Casualty 1907* (Stone City Films); *Liverpool One* (Lime Street Productions); *Heartbeat, Retrace, Emmerdale* (Yorkshire Television); *Wallander* (Left Bank Pictures).

Radio

Absolute Beginners, Stone (BBC Radio 4).

Film

A Boy Called Dad (Wonderboy Ltd.); *Starstruck* (Starstruck Films); *Trauma* (Trauma Productions); *The Calcium Kid* (Calcium Films Ltd); *Mean Machine* (SKA Mean Machine Ltd).

NICK MOSS
Agamemnon

ADAM REDMORE
Fury 2 / Chorus 2

Adam Redmore trained at the Royal Welsh College of Music and Drama.

Theatre
Serious Money (Waking Exploits); *Double Falsehood* (Union Theatre); *Dr Faustus, School for Scandal* (Greenwich Theatre); *Follow* (Finborough Festival); *Helianthus, Squat Party* (The Squat Collective).

Television
Doctors, Silent Witness (BBC Television); *The Bill* (Thames Television).

Radio
If You're Reading This, Under Milk Wood (BBC Radio 4).

Writing
Adam is a co-founding member of London based site-specific theatre company The Squat Collective. He co-wrote their last production *Helianthus*.

JONAH RUSSELL
Aegisthus

Theatre
Kursk (Sydney Opera House);
Yerma (West Yorkshire Playhouse);
Small Hours (Hampstead); *All The Things I'd Do For You* (Theatre Absolute); *Kursk* (Sound&Fury/ Young Vic); *Women of Troy, Attempts on Her Life, Waves, The Seagull, Pains of Youth* (National Theatre); *Waves* (Lincoln Center); *Romans in Britain* (Sheffield Crucible); *The Emperor Jones* (Gate); *Sergeant Musgrave's Dance, After the Dance* (Oxford Stage Company); *The Madness of George Dubya* (West End); *With Love From Nicolae* (Bristol Old Vic).

Television
Locked Up Abroad (Raw Television); *EastEnders, Doctors* (BBC Television); *The Bill* (Thames Television); *Green Wing, Melissa* (Channel 4); *Lucy Sullivan is Getting Married* (Carnival Productions).

Film
Stop the World, Missing, Hell's Pavement (Oopic Films); *Play the Game* (Alphapictures); *What a Girl Wants* (Warner Bros.); *Dog Eat Dog* (Tiger Aspect); *A Refugee.*

EIRY THOMAS
Chorus 1

Theatre
Measure for Measure (Sherman Cymru); *Soul Exchange* (National Theatre Wales); *Trojan Women, House of Bernarda Alba* (Theatr Pena); *Indian Country* (Sgript Cymru); *Talking Heads* (Sherman Theatre Company); *Skylight* (West Glamorgan Theatre).

Television & Film
Stella (Sky1); *Pentalar, Teulu, Gari Tryfan II, Con Passionate, Pobol y Cwm* (S4C); *EastEnders, Belonging, High Hopes, Torchwood, Casualty, The Bench, Lucky Bag* (BBC Television); *Cwcw* (Fondue Films).

Radio
From Fact to Fiction, Strike for a Kingdom, Don't Buy a Winter Coat, Oh Little Town of Aberystwyth, The Beacon, The Night Horse, No Refund for Clouds, Torchwood, Binge Drink Britain, Poems People Love, The Living Dead, Solomon, The LL Files, Under Milk Wood (BBC Radio).

Gwyneth Lewis
Writer

Gwyneth Lewis was the National Poet of Wales 2005-06, the first to be awarded the laureateship. Her words are on the front of the Wales Millennium Centre in six-foot-high letters, rumoured to be the largest poem in the world. In 2010 she was awarded a Society of Authors Cholmondeley Award for a distinguished body of work.

Gwyneth has published eight books of poems in Welsh and English, the latest being *Chaotic Angels*, *A Hospital Odyssey* and *Sparrow Tree*, all published by Bloodaxe. *Tair mewn Un* (Three in One) gathers her first three books in Welsh. Awards given to these books include the Aldeburgh Poetry Festival Prize and Cyngor Celfyddydau Cymru Llyfr y Flwyddyn. Gwyneth has published two books of non-fiction. *Sunbathing in the Rain: A Cheerful Book about Depression* (Harper Perennial) was adapted as a play for BBC Radio 4 and won a Mental Health in the Media award. She has written libretti for WNO MAX and a play about the principles of particle physics for BBC Radio 4's *Afternoon Play*.

Much of *Clytemnestra* was written in the US, where Gwyneth held fellowships at the Radcliffe Institute for Advanced Study at Harvard and the Stanford Humanities Center. Gwyneth was born, raised and lives in Cardiff.

Amy Hodge
Director

Amy was recipient of the Jerwood Directors Award 2007 and was Associate Director at Sherman Cymru 2008 – 2011. Amy will be directing *Rover* at Hampton Court Palace this summer.

Theatre
As Director: *Playing the Game* (Tricycle Theatre); *The Sanger, Light Arrested Between the Curtain and the Glass, Measure For Measure, A Christmas Carol, Small Change* (Sherman Cymru); *Mules* (Young Vic); *The Ethics of Progress* (Unlimited Theatre); *The Tempest, Kick For Touch* (Orange Tree Theatre); *Theatre Of Change* (West Yorkshire Playhouse); *The Vagina Monologues* (Leeds City Variety Music Hall).

As Assistant Director: *My Child, The Pain and the Itch* (Royal Court Theatre).

Peter Scott
Assistant Director

Peter Scott is currently being mentored by Elen Bowman and this is his first professional experience as an assistant director. Peter will shortly be developing a production of *Blavatsky's Tower* by Moria Buffini in association with Sherman Cymru's artist development programme.

takis
Designer

Theatre
His Teeth (Only Connect); *As You Like It, Merlin, Much Ado About Nothing, Hercules* (Chester Open Air Theatre); *Nicked, Midnight Your Time, Dusk Rings a Bell, Lidless* (HighTide/Edinburgh Festival); *Measure For Measure* (Sherman Cymru); *Oh What a Lovely War* (RADA); *Ditch* (Old Vic/HighTide); *The Early Bird* (Finborough Theatre/ Project Arts Centre, Dublin); *Signs of a Star Shaped Diva* (Theatre Royal Stratford East & National Tour); *Stovepipe* (National Theatre/HighTide); *The Marriage Bed* (Hong Kong/ NY); *Invasion* (Soho Theatre); *I Caught Crabs in Walberswick* (Bush Theatre & Edinburgh Festival); *Scenes from the Big Picture* (RADA); *Crazy Lady* (Drill Hall & Contact Theatre, Manchester); *Dick Whittington* (Gatehouse Theatre); *Nicked* (HighTide Festival); *A Tale of Two Cities* (Theatre Royal Brighton); *Bloodbath* (Edinburgh Festival); *Maria Callas - Vissi D'arte, Vissi D'amore* (Barbican); *Choruses, In the Light of the Night* (Ancient Epidaurus); *The Words of Love* (Athens); *Nikos Skalkotas* (Queen Elizabeth Hall).

Installations
Forgotten Peacock (Design Museum/ The Brunswick); *Installation 496* (RADA); *Goldfish* (Paris Fashion Week); *Mythological Installation Oedipus* (Bucharest Museum of Contemporary Art); *Visual Performance in Baroque Spirit* (Venice Carnival).

Film
Dreck (T-Squared Films); *Half Light, Eve* (Parkville Pictures).

Lee Curran
Lighting Designer

Theatre
Constellations (The Royal Court); *The Fat Girl Gets a Haircut* (Roundhouse); *Great Expectations* (English Touring Theatre/ Watford Palace); *Unbroken* (The Gate). Upcoming designs include *Toujours et Prés de Moi* (Opera Erratica); *66 Minutes in Damascus* (Lucien Bourjeily & LIFT Festival).

Dance
Political Mother, The Art of Not Looking Back, In Your Rooms, Uprising (Hofesh Shechter Company); *The Perfect Human* (CandoCo); *Curious Conscience* (Rambert Dance Company); *E2 7SD* (Rafael Bonachela); *From The Waist Up, Sticks and Bones* (Darren Ellis); *Have We Met Somewhere Before?* (PROBE); *Singing* (Jonathan Burrows Group). Upcoming designs include *The Impending Storm* (Mark Storer & International Festival of Dance Birmingham); a new work (Tony

Adigun/ Avante Garde Dance); two new works (James Cousins Dance).

Lee worked with Iain Forsythe & Jane Pollard on *An Evening with Nick Cave* and the music video *Dig, Lazarus, Dig!!!* He also works with the interdisciplinary design collective body>data>space in digital art, interactivity, space and the body.

Simon Thorne
Composer & Sound Designer

Simon Thorne lives and works in Cardiff. With Phillip Mackenzie he formed Man Act Theatre Company. Subsequently he has led The Canton Café Orchestra, playing Latin Jewish music, and jazz trio The Cherubs. With Paula Gardiner and Huw Warren he created the Wales Jazz Composers Orchestra.

Theatre
The Howl In Arcadia (Arts Council of Wales Creative Wales Major Award); *Hope Street* (part of Liverpool 2008 European City of Culture); *Neanderthal* (National Museum Wales); *The Infernal Twittering Machine* (Klangwerkstaat Weimar); *Magura* (Roumanian Village Soundscape); *Some Spaces (Empty Rooms)* (Cardiff University and Muzeul Judetean Teleormanul); *Ivan and the Wolf* (Welsh National Opera); *The Prodigy of Love*

(Concerto Gallese); *A Clockwork Orange* (Volcano Theatre).

Dr. Johan Stjernholm
Choreographer

Johan works as a freelance choreographer as well as a full-time Lecturer in Choreography and Performance at the Royal Academy of Dance in London. In 2003 he started up the Space Engineering Dance Company, an experimental collaborative venture that currently is based in London and performs internationally.

Johan's choreographic methods draw on his post-doctoral scholarly research on perception and embodiment, as well as his extensive practical engagement in various contemporary choreographic traditions. Situated at the crossroads between academia and performance practice, Johan works in close collaboration with some of the most prominent scholars and ground-breaking choreographers in the UK.

Johan received his PhD in Dance Studies from the University of the Arts London (UAL) in 2010. He graduated with an MA in European Dance Theatre Practice from Laban in 2003. In 2002 he finalised his BA (Hons.) Dance Theatre at Laban, London.

CLYTEMNESTRA

by Gwyneth Lewis

Place
A farm estate and related abattoir.

Setting
The Atreus family compound, the centre of a food business ruled by Agamemnon, who is away fighting a food war with competitors for the eastern market. Feral gangs roam the countryside outside.

Time
The near future, the world fights for food. Oil has nearly run out and the world has reverted to a tribal form of organization. Technology is only patchily sustainable so society looks like that of a much earlier time.

Characters in order of appearance

Cassandra: seer captured in Troy.

Proto-Furies: the Furies of Cassandra's family, killed by
            Agamemnon. They remain undeveloped pre-
            linguistic entities, though they may whisper
            some words, because Cassandra doesn't give
            them houseroom.

Agamemnon: head of the Atreus tribe, husband of
            Clytemnestra

Soldier:

Watchman:

Clytemnestra: wife of Agamemnon

Chorus: three individuals, of either sex, consisting of:

Chorus 1:   a foreman-type character
Chorus 2:   a middle-of-the-road person
Chorus 3:   the most down-to-earth, lazy one.

Furies: the ancient psychic force that demands
            avenging family murder. These figures have a
            primitive relationship with language but gain
            embodiment and change the more they're
            listened to. They start as pre-linguistic and pre-
            figurative and as the revenge idea develops,
            they come to resemble fully formed characters.
            When a character assents to them, they give
            that character a superhuman drive. They are

always trying to influence the play in the direction of revenge. The Furies stem from the oldest part of the brain, which responds to impulse, grudge. But they're also very energetic, rhythmic, they pulse with movement, they're dancers. They're the beat before rational thought. As such, they're the precursors and sponsors of poetic language. The Furies' voices should be more or less amplified and distorted, so that they sound slightly uncanny.

Fury 1: is the revenge backwash released by the murder of Iphigenia, daughter of Agamemnon and Clytemnestra.

Electra: daughter of Agamemnon and Clytemnestra.

Aegisthus: Agamemnon's cousin, member of the Thyestes tribe. Closer in age to Electra than Clytemnestra.

Fury 2: the force demanding revenge for the death of Aegisthus's brothers by Agamemnon's father.

ACT ONE

SCENE 1

Darkness. Lights up on CASSANDRA high on a parapet overlooking Troy, burning red below. As she speaks, she walks carefully up a sloping bar across the stage.

CASSANDRA:
From here, I can see everything:
The city's burning, such a pretty red.
She's the girl who cries wolf, they said.
I never. I just saw through time
To when I lose everything that's mine.

The PROTO-FURIES begin to play with and respond to CASSANDRA. She evades them, uses them to climb further up the city walls. Throughout this scene, the FURIES gradually take shape, abstract entities trying to gain a foothold in the human world.

So, now it starts. Walls come alive
And whisper: 'Revenge! You shan't rest.
Eye for an eye, tooth for a tooth.' (*She giggles.*)
Look! They want me! But that's not my game!
I've seen the gods and what they do.
I don't serve you. I see the future.

CASSANDRA plays and pokes with the emerging FURIES, like a child teasing an animal. She uses them to climb higher. Enter AGAMEMNON and SOLDIER.

SOLDIER:
I posted guards at all the granaries.
Shot a few looters, sent out word we share
Supplies with any one who helps us trade.
The policy, like you said is: firm but fair.

The FURIES produce a figure representing IPHIGENIA in white near CASSANDRA.

AGAMEMNON:
All this way for food.

CASSANDRA:
     Agamemnon,
Are you happy now?

AGAMEMNON starts, looks up, sees the IPHIGENIA figure, cries out.

AGAMEMNON:
     Iphigenia!

CASSANDRA:
No! Cassandra.

SOLDIER:
    Sniper! Take cover!

CASSANDRA:
Agamemnon, the Furies want you dead
But I refuse. I've got things I want to say
To you . . . You have to listen. No, get off me!
Once you act, you see much less.

CASSANDRA stands up precariously on the parapet, the FURIES' hands try to hold on to her.

AGAMEMNON:

Don't fall!

CASSANDRA falls from the wall, the FURIES wail. AGAMEMNON catches her.

Hold your fire! It's just a girl.
I've got you, love. You're fine. I've got you.

AGAMEMNON cradles her.

SCENE 2

Atreus compound at night. Torchlight.

WATCHMAN:
Time was, I'd look out and see lights,
Farms sailing through the night like ships,
Brave in the black. That was before
The end of oil, wars for food.
The dark has overwhelmed us. Shush!
What's that? It's hunger in the hedge. (*Dims his torch.*)
Eyes watch us, ferals lick their lips.
Their teeth are sharp. Agamemnon's gone
Out east for food. I'm like a dog – my eyes are drawn
In his direction, bored with everything
That isn't him. I watch for signs –
A bonfire – that he's on his way.
First to see it gets a prize.
Good night so far, not much to see,
But I heard plenty.

A light goes up in the house, CLYTEMNESTRA groans.

              Clytemnestra.
Makes my blood run cold. . . Bad business,
That. She doesn't sleep because
Her daughter's dead. Iphigenia,
Whose father, Agamemnon sent
For her. He got her all mixed up
In some dark deal for food. She died.
I'm glad I'm just an ordinary man.
Who'd be a leader? Better far
To be a pleb. They say the gods

4

Are dead, I'm not so sure. What we've
Become's another matter. Dawn at last.

He rubs his eyes, puts out the torch.

Agamemnon didn't come tonight.
I'm on the early shift. The final kill.
And then we're out of meat. When men
Are hungry then we'll see what's what.

SCENE 3

The kill floor. CHORUS 1, 2 and 3 starting a shift.

CHORUS 2:
But it doesn't make sense to slaughter the last
Of the herd!

CHORUS 1:
            Those are my orders.

CHORUS 2:
Think of it, man. What happens next spring
No milk, no suckling calves?

CHORUS 3:
                            The woman's
Lost it!

CHORUS 1:
            Don't you start!

CHORUS 2:
Agreed. Madam thinks far more
About her dead daughter than her living clan.

CHORUS 1:
She's Clytemnestra to the likes of you.
Move it! Let's get this show on the road.

CHORUS 3:
The ladies are in. Stringy lot.
Bony backs and floppy teats.

CHORUS 2:
Not much of a mouthful there for us.
Still, the bones will make broth for the kids.

CHORUS 1:
Stunner, shackler, let's be having you.

CHORUS 2:
And how do you expect us to kill
On empty stomachs? We're working men!

CHORUS 3:
I'm all shaky, can hardly stand.
Look at me! I'm thin
As a rake. Run out of notches on my belt.

He pulls out his baggy trousers.

CHORUS 2:
It's their job to feed us. Otherwise
What good are they?

CHORUS 1:
                    Shut it!
I won't have that talk on the kill floor.
Agamemnon's on the way with food.
That's all you need to know. Everything hangs
On that.

CHORUS 2:
            Well, he's taking his time.

CHORUS 1:
Once we start, I don't want to stop.

CHORUS 3:
No, the line doesn't stop for anything.

CHORUS 1:
Right, let's go!

The generator fires up and the men make their way to their places.

CHORUS 3: (*to CHORUS 2*)
God! I'm hung-over.

CHORUS 2:
                    Been at the moonshine
Again?

CHORUS 3:
Spreading a little joy, that's all.

CHORUS 2:
You? A woman? Never!

CHORUS 3: (*nodding at CLYTEMNESTRA*)
Someone needs comfort.

CHORUS 2:
                    What, the boss's wife?

CHORUS 3:
Agamemnon's been away so long
She's gagging for it!

Throughout this conversation, the men are pulling levers, starting machines.

> She's had it rough,
Mind you, losing her kid like that.

CHORUS 2:
What are you talking about? If it were up to her
We'd all be starving. I know it was horrible,
But without the blood pact, where would we be?
Times are rough. The world's not civilized.

CHORUS 3:
Harder on some than others.

CHORUS 1:
I think you'll find: Food first and morals later.

CHORUS 3: (*making sure CHORUS 1 doesn't hear*)
They say the ferals are moving closer.
Been seen by the river. By day. As brass.

CHORUS 2:
When we've killed all the animals,
Men will be next.

CHORUS 1:
> Look sharp!

*Each member of the CHORUS wields a different piece of
equipment. The first worker stuns the cattle as they come in.
The second shackles each animal's leg and hoists it up,
slitting the animal's throat. The third wields a rotary band
saw to cut up the carcass. They each start individually in
sequence, building up to a whole rhythmic machine, a
percussive collage. As the men begin work, enter
CLYTEMNESTRA followed at a distance by FURY 1.*

CHORUS 1:
The Jarvis Model CZSS1 is a pneumatically operated
penetrating high-speed captive Bolt Stunner for cattle. Its
single-shot stunning action humanely renders animals
insensitive to pain.

*He repeats the action of stunning the cattle and occasionally
interrupting himself to say his private thought, and this
progresses into a dance.*

When the bolt is lowered for me,
Let me not see it.

*He steps back and continues under the others as they join in.
From time to time he steps out and speaks his secret thought.
Each member of the chorus repeats this pattern, building up a
choreographed slaughterhouse production line. CHORUS 2
lifts each cow by her leg and, shackling her to the gantry above,
steadies the swinging body so that the next man can cut the
carcass. The action is oddly reminiscent of a reassuring pat
you might give a child.*

CHORUS 2:
The Beef Hock Restrainer Model BHR-1, eliminates kill
floor down time required for re-hanging fallen carcasses.
Rugged stainless steel and galvanized construction for
long, trouble-free operation.

He steps out into his dream thought.

Just as long as the one killed today
Isn't me.

He slashes the throat of each cow before the body moves on.

CHORUS 3 is using a bandsaw to cut the hanging carcass in half.

CHORUS 3:
The Jarvis Buster 5 Line Dropper has a superior blade life, four- to six-hundred carcasses. Designed to reduce operator fatigue, this baby has a totally enclosed motor for fast cleanup.

CHORUS 3:
No matter how much I scrub my nails,
Bloodstains won't shift.

Towards the end of this routine, which is played to a background of industrial steam noises and loud running water, something in white, which looks like a young girl is passed down the production line. CLYTEMNESTRA looks on in horror, not knowing if she's imagining it or not, but she's seeing IPHIGENIA being murdered. The men act as if nothing is out of the ordinary. As the routine reaches its climax, CLYTEMNESTRA screams and rushes onto to the kill floor, which is now bathed in red, bringing work to a halt.

CLYTEMNESTRA:
No! Stop! I won't allow it!

Startled, the men stop and somebody cuts the power. Everybody looks at each other in horror, the whole process of producing food stopped in its tracks. Lights out.

SCENE 4

CLYTEMNESTRA's still sobbing on a couch, mid-stage.
She's whimpering in terror. ELECTRA comforts her. To the
left, spotlight on IPHIGENIA'S ashes in a plastic bag. While
we're distracted by the conversation between CLYTEMNESTRA
and ELECTRA, as if out of the floor, FURY 1 rises as her
incantation becomes audible. She should be curled in a crescent
around the ashes. Throughout this scene, the FURY repeats the
words given.

FURY 1: (*going from sub-audible to audible during the course*
of the scene)
Ullulloo . . . leela loo . . . wellaloo . . .
Eararam . . . loolaram . . . eraram . . .
Orreeree . . . erarie, oorarree.
Werrarrat . . . orrarrat . . . errerree . . .

CLYTEMNESTRA:
I saw them kill her again! My baby!

ELECTRA:
Mum, I told you to stay inside,
Away from the kill floor. It's common sense,
You're still in shock.

CLYTEMNESTRA:
                                        Leave me alone!

ELECTRA:
I know you're grieving but keep it in here!

CLYTEMNESTRA:
How can you be so hard about your sister?

ELECTRA:
Our feelings mean nothing. We can't let the men
See what a state we're in.

*By now FURY 1 is fully materialized by the ashes. At a gesture
from her a beam of light rises from the bag, as tall as a person.
The FURY begins to throw up dust, to make the column
moresubstantial. CLYTEMNESTRA responds instinctively,
reaching for her, as if her daughter was appearing before her.*

CLYTEMNESTRA:
I can't see anything else but her. In my mind
I play it over and over.

FURY 1: (*this chant weaves through the dialogue*)
Love her . . . lover . . . love her to death they did
Lover her . . . on top of her . . . top of . . . under her

over her . . .

To death lover her to death they did . . .
In her . . . ow! round her . . . all roundabout her . . .

ELECTRA:
The men have got to understand
That although my father's away from home,
He's still in charge.

CLYTEMNESTRA:
Agamemnon! He doesn't deserve to live.

ELECTRA:
Come on,
He must have done the best for us . . .

CLYTEMNESTRA rouses herself and, for the first time, the sounds made by the FURY and her speech begins to relate to each other. It isn't clear at this point who leads and who follows.

CLYTEMNESTRA:
It plays like a loop in my head. The way
He handed her over to that tribe
Like a prize . . .

ELECTRA:
                You weren't even there,
Give him some credit!

CLYTEMNESTRA:
                I see it, feel it: the dirty nails,
They smell of drink. And he gave my child
As part of a trade. For food!

ELECTRA:
Till he gets back we can't be sure
Exactly what happened . . .

FURY 1:
Wrong, this is wrong, can't not remember (*repeated*)

CLYTEMNESTRA:
Your father's wiped me off the face of the earth.

ELECTRA:
Look at me! Listen! The men could turn
In a second and throw us out
Of the compound. Ferals hunt
In packs out there.

CLYTEMNESTRA:
I couldn't care less!

FURY 1:
Member . . . re-remember . . .

CLYTEMNESTRA:
When Iphigenia
Was born the vessels in my eyes
Burst like plums. I saw her first
Through a film of blood.

ELECTRA:
What can I do
To help?

Throughout CLYTEMNESTRA's speech, the FURY crawls towards her on her belly.

CLYTEMNESTRA:
Every day's slaughter in my mind.

ELECTRA:
Then why did you go to the kill floor?

FURY 1:
Wrung out . . . so strung out . . . won't not remember . . .

CLYTEMNESTRA: *(to FURY 1)*
So tell me what I have to do.

ELECTRA: *(mistaking the addressee)*
You should eat. No wonder you're worn out,
It's been days since you tasted anything. Try some of this.

ELECTRA feeds CLYTEMNESTRA some meat. The FURY recoils and CLYTEMNESTRA appears stronger.

See? You were hungry. There. That's it.
Look, something went wrong out East.
Maybe the party was betrayed,
You know how quickly things turn bad
When you're dealing with strangers – ferals
With trade routes. There. You look better already.
Will you get up?

ELECTRA walks between CLYTEMNESTRA and the FURY, who withdraws from her as if she were fire.

CLYTEMNESTRA:
              Electra, I'm losing my mind. I see . . .
Such horrors.

ELECTRA:
              Give it time.
I've got you. I promise I'll see us through.
This is your home, a safe place to fall.
You can hold on to me. Now rest a while.

Sharp knocking at the door. At this distraction, the FURY regains momentum and manages to reach and touch CLYTEMNESTRA.

FURY 1:
Wrong, did no wrong, did no wrong . . .
Hear tendons tear . . . tendons tear, tendons twisting . . .

ELECTRA:
Hell! It's the men. They'll want to know
What happened down there. What shall I say?

CLYTEMNESTRA:
I can't think . . . There are other voices . . .

*FURY 1 now has CLYTEMNESTRA'S attention and dictates
what she thinks.*

ELECTRA:
You're scaring me now.

CLYTEMNESTRA:
                                        Their filthy fingers . . .

FURY 1:
Right, had no right . . . to find rape delicious!

*CLYTEMNESTRA's lips move to the FURY's words. Second
knock.*

CHORUS 1: (*offstage*)
Hello? You there?

ELECTRA: (*moving towards the door, looking back*)
They won't listen to me.

CHORUS 1: (*more aggressively*)
We know you're in there!

ELECTRA:
Quickly! Tell me what I should do.

FURY 1:
He did it . . . he did it . . . Agamemnon did it . . .

CLYTEMNESTRA:
Do what you like! I've got other business . . .

ELECTRA:
This is important! If they rebel
We won't survive!

CLYTEMNESTRA:
                    I want my daughter!

ELECTRA:
I'm here, I told you!

*More knocking. FURY leads CLYTEMNESTRA towards the
column of dust.*

CLYTEMNESTRA:
                    I don't want you
Or your sister's ashes. I want Iphigenia.

FURY 1:
'Sallright, 'sallright, 'sallright, 'sallright now,
She'll come . . . she'll come . . . she'll come to mamma . . .

Third knock.

CHORUS 1:
We know you're inside! We need to talk!

*ELECTRA moves towards the door hesitant, turning back
to look at CLYTEMNESTRA and the FURY.
CLYTEMNESTRA'S embracing the column of dust.
ELECTRA collects herself, opens the door, light floods in
on her.*

ELECTRA:
How dare you make all this noise? Get back to work!
My mother's resting. I won't have her disturbed
By the likes of you. I want to hear
The kill floor working or you'll answer to me.
That line doesn't stop for anything. No.
The line doesn't stop for anything.

SCENE 5

On the journey. AGAMEMNON watching CASSANDRA
hunched down, facing the audience, preoccupied. Behind her the
PROTO-FURIES dance, as they're never absent from the world
that she sees.

AGAMEMNON:
How old are you, darling? About the same age as . . .
Iphigenia . . .

He smells her hand and is felled by the reminder of his daughter.
CASSANDRA lets him, as if her mind is distinct from her
body.

        So many years of travelling, fighting.
I've had no time to think. Till this. Now you.
A young girl's wrist . . . Such tiny bones,
So easily broken. I thought they'd cherish
Her. She went a bride, came back a corpse.

CASSANDRA: (*in a totally calm, authoritative voice*)
No rest for the good. It's only starting.

AGAMEMNON: (*recoiling and dropping her hand*)
What?

CASSANDRA:
        Now all the corpses get up, the carpet
Sticky from under them, they want revenge.

AGAMEMNON: (*draws a knife*)
Don't move.

CASSANDRA:
They want me to kill you but I won't.

AGAMEMNON:
Stay there! Can't believe I let down my guard.

CASSANDRA:
They're hard to bear, droning on and on.

Addressing the Furies.

Oh change the topic!

AGAMEMNON:
                          No, she's touched.

CASSANDRA:
I hear you, yes, I hear you . . . Shoo!

AGAMEMNON:
                          Look at me.

CASSANDRA: (*disobeying*)
They've told me what they have in mind for you.
The Furies want to write my part for me.
I'm refusing.

AGAMEMNON:
                          I'm in charge.

*CASSANDRA giggles. AGAMEMNON's at a loss as to
what to do with her.*

CASSANDRA:

You really think it's you?
The blood choir's here, they're staging a play
About vengeance. Their plot is: I'm to kill
The man who destroyed my city and who
Sacrificed his daughter.

AGAMEMNON:

I was right!

CASSANDRA:
They don't think so.

AGAMEMNON:

Who are you talking to?

CASSANDRA:
The ones who want us in the light to do
Their dirty work, the vengeance mothers.

AGAMEMNON: (*wearily*)
I get it. Seen too many things. You poor,
Poor girl.

CASSANDRA:

No, silly! I'm the lucky one,
I get to *see* how it works, the slides and pulleys
That pivot the future. Nothing to do with right
Or wrong. It's just what part you choose to play
And why.

AGAMEMNON:

Morals are everything. The head
Of a clan must do what's best for all his people.

CASSANDRA:
If it suits him . . .

AGAMEMNON:
He puts his personal feelings
Aside for the general good.

CASSANDRA:
It hasn't done me
Any good.

AGAMEMNON:
My job's to do what has
To be done, no matter what –

CASSANDRA:
You've killed me. As you
Killed your daughter.

AGAMEMNON hits her, so she falls over.

AGAMEMNON:
I did wrong
For the right reasons. You, a prisoner,
Don't question me . . .

CASSANDRA:
Why not? I've nothing left
To lose. I'll say whatever I want.

AGAMEMNON:
I could . . .

CASSANDRA:
I'm nothing now. Nobody's daughter. I
Could disappear and nobody would notice.

*FURIES surround CASSANDRA, push her to knees, she
becomes very distressed.*

No more blood. You've had too much already.
Ah! Don't leave me with them!

AGAMEMNON:
                              Victor and victim,
Doesn't seem to matter. No one has peace
Of mind. I guarantee that I'll protect you.

CASSANDRA:
Don't you see? That's the point. You can't.

Lights out.

SCENE 6

*CLYTEMNESTRA lies in bed, eyes open, staring at the
ashes. FURY 1 paces around the room. She's more embodied,
her face now has a mouth. Throughout this scene, there
should be a physical link reflecting the growing field of
connection between CLYTEMNESTRA and the FURY.*

FURY 1:
Who'll speak for the dead girls if I don't?
The teenagers with skinny shoulders,
Out in party dresses, no coats,
The bodies are found on waste ground later,
Strangled with their own tights.

CLYTEMNESTRA:
Leave me alone!

FURY 1:
⠀⠀⠀⠀⠀⠀⠀⠀⠀⠀You see them in photos,
Bad haircuts, teeth too large, clothes
Chosen by Mum.

CLYTEMNESTRA:
⠀⠀⠀⠀⠀⠀⠀⠀⠀⠀Sleep, I need sleep . . .

FURY 1:
She'll follow you there. She's looking for you,
Where were you? Sit up so we can talk!

CLYTEMNESTRA doubles up in pain.

CLYTEMNESTRA:
I must have done wrong . . . I'm being punished.
I wasn't maternal, I should have cuddled . . .

FURY 1:
Me seems to recall, the Nestie not wanty
Girls . . .

CLYTEMNESTRA:
       Too clingy . . .

FURY 1:
                    Boys much better . . . Mum knows
Where she is with them . . .

CLYTEMNESTRA:
           No!
That's not quite right . . . The kids would go
To Agamemnon if they were hurt . . . We used to laugh
About it.

FURY 1:
        Did Clytemnestra mind?
She said she didn't.

CLYTEMNESTRA:
          But I did.
I heard their voices soften when
They played with him, they giggled more.

FURY 1:
So sentimental. Words are easy,
I deal in facts. Whom did she resemble?

CLYTEMNESTRA:
Everyone said she looked like me.

FURY 1:
She wasn't his to give, she was yours!
Did Clytemnestra care for them when they were ill?

CLYTEMNESTRA:
I did!

FURY 1:
Who was it took her into danger?

CLYTEMNESTRA:
Agamemnon! Clytemnestra is
The better parent!

FURY 1:
Did Clytemnestra
Kill no, rape, then kill her daughter?
He took her from you.

CLYTEMNESTRA:
No man should come
Between mother and daughter.

FURY 1:
Love her to death they did . . . they fucked her
Fucked her till they broke her.

CLYTEMNESTRA lunges for the ashes.

CLYTEMNESTRA:
My daughter. Iphigenia, come home
To Clytemnestra's body, which is warm.

CLYTEMNESTRA crams ashes into her mouth.

FURY 1:
Now the whole drama comes into focus:
How shall we make Agamemnon pay?
There is a neighbour can come out to play,
In a worse state than you, he living in slurry.
Two messed-up clans that fucked each other
For fun and vengeance over years and years.

Enter ELECTRA.

ELECTRA:
What are you doing? Oh for pity's sake . . .

ELECTRA rushes over to hold her mother, to rock her.
CLYTEMNESTRA continues to struggle, trying to hear
what the FURY's proposing.

FURY 1:
Aegisthus. Go calling on him. Agamemnon's
Cousin. He'll understand,
He'll be your friend . . .

CLYTEMNESTRA:
Daughters always belong to mothers.

ELECTRA:
Oh, Clytemnestra.

Behind them, the FURY expresses satisfaction in small insect
movements.

SCENE 7

CHORUS 1, 2 and 3 eating after their shift. Behind them the kill floor machinery is clean. CHORUS 3 tips his lunch bag into his mouth to catch the last of the crumbs.

CHORUS 1:
Careful, man, you'll be eating the bag.

CHORUS 3:
Damned right I will. This wasn't enough.
I'm starving.

CHORUS 2:
                    What part of a cow
Was this when it was alive? It's tough
As leather.

Throws it away in disgust. CHORUS 3 picks it up.

CHORUS 3:
            I'll have it.

CHORUS 1:
                        Ugh!

CHORUS 3:
                        'S all right!
I'd rather have meat than bloody barley
And this is the last of it.

CHORUS 2:
                    Enjoy!

So lads, now we come down to basics.
No meat. Is Clytemnestra up to it?

CHORUS 1:
What are you on about now?

CHORUS 2:
                                        The question
Is this: can Clytemnestra feed us?

CHORUS 1:
Give it a rest. It's not for you . . .

CHORUS 3:
They're on borrowed time, the lot of them.

CHORUS 1:
The clan's been fine to us so far.

CHORUS 3:
Good to themselves, more like. Remember,
They have to eat, too! They sling us offal
While they eat steak.

CHORUS 1:
                                That's not right.
Lord Agamemnon –

CHORUS 3:
                                Hark at him! Lord Agamemnon!
Your 'umble slave, can I lick your plate? –

CHORUS 1 takes an abattoir knife and holds it to
CHORUS 3's throat.

CHORUS 1:
Don't ever let me hear you make fun
Of him like that, he's risked his life
To find us supplies.

CHORUS 2:
               Cool it, boys!
Everyone's hungry, on a short fuse . . .

CHORUS 3:
The meat's all gone. Man wasn't meant
To be veggie.

CHORUS 1 backs down reluctantly.

CHORUS 2:
Clytemnestra held it together
As Flesh Divider, she was fair.

CHORUS 3:
Don't be daft! That was all Electra
Behind her. The woman's a wreck.

CHORUS 2:
Come on now, can you blame her?

CHORUS 1:
Not this again! He had to do it
They're savages out East, you play
By their rules and they require
Blood treaties.

CHORUS 3:
              Would you give
Your daughter to bandits? To fuck her? To death?

CHORUS 1: (*really uncomfortable*)
You have to think of the general good.

CHORUS 3:
You pompous prick. You don't rear kids
For the 'general good.' What he did was inhuman.

CHORUS 1:
So you won't be eating any supplies
He sends us?

CHORUS 2:
        What supplies?

CHORUS 3:
Exactly! Oh, they talk and talk about what's to come
But where *is* it? If I had my way
I'd be rid of the lot.

CHORUS 1:
        You've got to give them time.

CHORUS 2:
If Agamemnon isn't back soon
With food this compound will crash.

CHORUS 3:
Hell, I bet the ferals have more on their plates
Than we do. And *that* would be fresh.

CHORUS 1:
If what I've heard about them is true
They'd welcome a visit from you.

CHORUS 2:
                                                 They start
On the thighs, work their way up . . .

CHORUS 3:
There's nothing of me . . .

CHORUS 2:
                                     . . . to the sweetmeats!

CHORUS 3:
Geddoff!

CHORUS 1:
                   Go on, leave! See
How you like nettles and berries. No,
I didn't think so.

CHORUS 3:
                     Look at this gear!
It's nothing but an ornament!

CHORUS 1:
You'll hear it sing again when Agamemnon
Gets back with food.

CHORUS 2:
                      We won't have long to wait
To see what's what.

Exeunt CHORUS 2 and CHORUS 3

CHORUS 1:
People change when they're really hungry.
Flesh and blood aside, we'll see
What parents will do when they're out of meat.

SCENE 8

*AEGISTHUS'S house. FURY 2 opens the door to FURY 1 who
leads in CLYTEMNESTRA by the hand. AEGISTHUS is
cowering on the floor, with FURY 2 over him. Both FURIES
have a magnetic field that drags CLYTEMNESTRA and
AEGISTHUS respectively in their wakes, though AEGISTHUS
is less responsive.*

CLYTEMNESTRA:
Hello? Aegisthus? The door was open.
It's Agamemnon's wife, your cousin . . .
Nobody in. What a mess. Looks like
Ferals have raided . . .

AEGISTHUS groans.

FURY 1:
                          Serve we not
The cause of rage? Of grudge?

FURY 2:
Tit-for-tat retaliation!
Making the other one hurt! Revenge!

The FURIES kiss, taste each other.

FURY 1:
My lot made his father consume
His sons!

FURY 2:
             No wonder this one
Can't eat.

FURY 1:

>Food's good!

FURY 2:

>>Not when
It ruined his father, and the curse
Of such humiliation still sickens him.

CLYTEMNESTRA:
What happened to you?

FURY 2:

>>I'm intent
On shedding blood for blood.
He must kill Agamemnon.

CLYTEMNESTRA:

>>I can
Help, Aegisthus.

FURY 2 forces AEGISTHUS to look at CLYTEMNESTRA.

FURY 2:

>>He blocks me at every
Turn. He never co-operates.
And yours?

FURY 1:

>Coming on nicely.

FURY 2:

>>My puppet
Has tangled strings. He weighs a ton.

CLYTEMNESTRA:
Stand up so I can see you, come on!

Both FURIES haul AEGISTHUS to his feet.

FURY 2:
I can make grown men eat soil!
But this one . . .

FURY 1:
He is indeed full tardy.

AEGISTHUS:
I stink. Haven't washed in a while.

CLYTEMNESTRA: (*sniffs*)
I can't smell anything bad. You're fine.

AEGISTHUS:
It's rank like rotting food. Blocked drains.

CLYTEMNESTRA:
Calm yourself.

AEGISTHUS:
Who asked you to come?

FURY 2:
You did, that be exactly what we done:
We called her, tempted, wished her over . . .

CLYTEMNESTRA:
Did family do this to you?

AEGISTHUS: (*breaking down*)
I've tried and tried to hide this stuff.
At night it comes from the taps . . . My hands
Are raw from scrubbing. It just . . .Keeps coming . . .
Shame for not being what my father . . .
Wants . . . So weak . . . I disgust myself.

CLYTEMNESTRA:
You've been crushed by the clan. I understand.

AEGISTHUS:
Anything I do just makes it worse.

CLYTEMNESTRA:
                                        I'll help you.

AEGISTHUS:
You can't. I'm . . .
Damned. Leave me alone.

CLYTEMNESTRA:
I already lost a daughter
I should have hid her, cut her hair,
Disguised her as a boy but no,
I let her join the campaign for food,
Thought she'd be safe with her father. And now
All I eat and breathe and drink
Is her and she's dust.

FURY 2:
                                        I want revenge on Agamemnon.
Nobody kills this tribe and lives.
The father's gone. I want Agamemnon
Dead for his crime.

FURY 1:
> Sister, well met!
For once we have the perfect rhyme,
Two Furies, one murder on their minds.

FURY 1 begins to sing and FURY 2 joins in.

AEGISTHUS:
My mind says terrible things to me.
As if my blood were dreaming revenge
I get no rest from that whine, it grates . . .

CLYTEMNESTRA:
You hear it too?

AEGISTHUS:
It makes me want to claw off my skin.
You mean I'm not mad?

CLYTEMNESTRA:
> No more than I am.
What if we both ignored them?
We've suffered enough . . . Isn't it time
We had some peace?

AEGISTHUS:
Some damage can never be undone.

CLYTEMNESTRA:
Shh . . . We're safe together. We
Can beat them.
Long moment of stillness, listening, not moving.

AEGISTHUS:
You're right. Already my head feels clearer. (*Giggles.*)

CLYTEMNESTRA:
So the voices?

AEGISTHUS:
Gone!

*He stands up, as if trying his body out again. He pulls
CLYTEMNESTRA to her feet.*

AEGISTHUS:
Soft hands.

CLYTEMNESTRA:
You're welcome.

FURY 2:
Ah, sweet.

FURY 1:
She's coming in baby steps,
A little more playing and I'm in.

*The FURIES' insect sounds develop into a song. AEGISTHUS
and CLYTEMNESTRA dance slowly at first, then more
energetically, a dance of relief, freedom and connection.
Through the dance the FURIES guide them like puppets.
As the dance reaches a climax, FURIES exchange a high five.*

SCENE 9

*The kill floor. Enter CLYTEMNESTRA like a queen with
FURIES 1 and 2 and AEGISTHUS like a retinue behind her.
CHORUS observing.*

CLYTEMNESTRA:
Our problems are solved. I have excellent news.

ELECTRA:
Agamemnon!

CLYTEMNESTRA:
             No. Something . . . better.

ELECTRA:
Who's that?

CLYTEMNESTRA:
             I'll beg you to show
Respect to Aegisthus, our latest partner.
I've made a new strategic alliance
With him and he will secure this compound
All it needs.

ELECTRA: (*hurrying CLYTEMNESTRA to one side*)
             You *can't* do this
Without consulting with me. I've run
This place while you've been . . . ill.

CLYTEMNESTRA:
I'm better now.

ELECTRA:
How can you be?
Something's happened, I don't understand.
Aegisthus? The son of our enemy?

AEGISTHUS:
That's no way to talk to your cousin.

ELECTRA:
Your father put himself outside
Being family . . .

CLYTEMNESTRA:
Forget the past.

AEGISTHUS:
Times are hard. Neighbours should help.

ELECTRA:
I can't forget my father's feud.

CLYTEMNESTRA:
My dear, you've done well with the rations
While I was . . . But now I'm ready
To take full charge and run the compound.

ELECTRA: (*talking to her mother-to-daughter*)
What's happened? Something's different!

CLYTEMNESTRA:
Hunger, that's what! It's been five days
Since we finished the meat. We were dead
If I hadn't found us new supplies.

ELECTRA:
This isn't the way. You cannot trust
This man. He wants our family dead!

CLYTEMNESTRA: (*the fury roused in her, with a threat of violence*)
Don't take that tone with me, or you
Can leave.

ELECTRA:
      For God's . . .

CLYTEMNESTRA:
            Don't think I won't.
The ferals would love another woman.
Agamemnon's bringing nothing back.
Do you seriously think
That a man who killed his favourite daughter
Would give a second thought for home?
No. We've waited long enough.
I, Clytemnestra, have taken action
And saved our hides. Inside you'll find
A new consignment.

ELECTRA:
      From where?

AEGISTHUS:
My compound. My supplies.

CLYTEMNESTRA:
Everything we need and more.

CHORUS brings in blue plastic barrels.

This is for all of you. From now on
I'm head of this clan, not Agamemnon.
And here is my chosen man, Aegisthus.
You said you were hungry. Here's your food.
I act and find I draw all eyes
To me. Flies swarm to meat, wasps drink
The sweet bruised flesh of apples till
They reel. I know who I am at last
And vow to follow it to the end.
Come here. I'm hungry – not for food –
But for an audience and you.

She drags off AEGISTHUS still being pushed by FURY 2.

CHORUS 1:
I'm so hungry I don't care
Where this is from.

ELECTRA:
                It isn't right.

CHORUS 3:
Suppose we just taste it so see what it's like?
In the interest of science?

CHORUS 1:
Think of the children.

CHORUS 3:
                Try and stop me.

CHORUS 3 opens a barrel. Stink hits them. Lights down.

ACT TWO

SCENE 1

AGAMEMNON and CASSANDRA on a beach. PROTO-FURIES are in a much less developed form than in CLYTEMNESTRA and AEGISTHUS scenes, more like sirens, but they're moved on from the first CASSANDRA scene. They're musical.

AGAMEMNON:
That's where we used to dive for scallops when
The kids were small. We're on the last leg home.

CASSANDRA:
I want to explore.

AGAMEMNON:
                    All right, but not for long.
We must keep pushing on. Clytemnestra
Will be waiting.

CASSANDRA begins to walk on water. The PROTO-FURIES may be supporting her feet.

                    The girls loved coming here
To hunt for crabs and starfish in the pools . . .

CASSANDRA:
Shadows. Seaweed, little darting fish.

AGAMEMNON:
Be careful, those rocks are sharp. Don't fall.

CASSANDRA:
Oh!

AGAMEMNON:
Cass, be careful. What can you see?

CASSANDRA:

                                    Shapes
That move like dreams. They're looming.

AGAMEMNON:
Iphigenia, come back! You've gone too far!

CASSANDRA:
No! not nearly far enough! Fish eye
Sees me through silver foil, oh
Furies aren't only here, they're coming to meet us,
Up out of the weeds, they're hungry mouths.

AGAMEMNON:
Whatever you do now don't look down. Keep calm.

CASSANDRA:
He says don't look! But now the sea
Swirls bloody beneath, that crimson's mine and his!
Sea salt, blood salts, blood sea.

AGAMEMNON:
I told you, don't look down!

CASSANDRA:

                        I close my eyes,
But I have see-through lids, I use my hands,
They're see-through. Furies reach through my body,

I'm nothing but a few degrees of warm
In the surrounding cold.

*AGAMEMNON seeing her frozen, moves out along the horizon
towards CASSANDRA.*

AGAMEMNON:
Look at me, Cassie! Sweetheart, that's right. Turn round.
Good girl, move towards me slowly.

CASSANDRA:
Nothing will save us. We're going to die.

*AGAMEMNON looks down, sees IPHIGENIA figure
underwater, slipping away from him.*

Tide swerves, blow follows blow. (*Addressing FURIES*) I still
refuse,
I'll watch you do your worst, it's not my worst.

AGAMEMNON:
No! . . . I didn't want to let her go!
Doesn't that make it right?

*CASSANDRA and FURIES sing a wordless phrase together.
CASSANDRA moves carefully towards AGAMEMNON, who's
utterly undone, takes his hand and guides him ashore.*

CASSANDRA:
Trust me, look up! It's me. You did you best.
Let's sit a while and listen to the sea.

They lean on each other. Sound of waves.

SCENE 11

*Night-time. The FERALS can be heard. CHORUS members
have hand-held torches.*

CHORUS 3:
Nothing?

CHORUS 2:
Nothing.

*CHORUS 1 and 3 turn to the audience, faces in searchlights,
and voice their fears.*

CHORUS 1:
Everything's wrong. Our food is poisoned.
Soon we'll be turning on one another
Like animals grown savage with hunger.

CHORUS 3:
Teeth tear at me in the dark, I'm eaten alive.

They carry on looking out for Agamemnon.

CHORUS 3: (*to CHORUS 2 but 1 hears*)
There's no point staying.

CHORUS 2:
                                    He's coming.

CHORUS 3:
You're even thicker than you look.
All you can see is feral fires.
Agamemnon's lying in a ditch, throat slit.

CHORUS 1:
Anyone caught absconding will lose
Their family's shares from their compound stores
Now and in perpetuity.

CHORUS 3:
That means: one seventy-sixth of nothing!

CHORUS 2:
Nothing's much better than that bloody food
Aegisthus brought. It gave me the shits,
The baby's still not over it.

CHORUS 3:
She's off her head, she'll kill us all!

CHORUS 1:
There shouldn't be a change of leader
Without us agreeing.

CHORUS grows desperate.

CHORUS 2:
I'm seeing spots because of hunger
But look over there.

CHORUS 1:
A bonfire. The signal we arranged.

CHORUS 2:
You see it too? It's not just me?

CHORUS 3:
The boss is coming! Agamemnon's
On his way with food!

CHORUS 1:
>   Go to the house,
> Tell them the good news right away.

Exit CHORUS 3.

CHORUS 1:
Agamemnon's coming home!

Lights down.

SCENE 12

AEGISTHUS on the kill floor. Enter ELECTRA.

ELECTRA:
What are you doing here?

AEGISTHUS:
                              I could ask the same
Of you.

ELECTRA:
          My home. You don't belong.

AEGISTHUS:
Your mother thinks I do. Besides,
You need my food.

ELECTRA:
                              That stuff
Is rotting.

AEGISTHUS:
          They took it.

ELECTRA:
                              I noticed
You didn't touch it.

AEGISTHUS:
                    No appetite.

The two sidle around each other warily, touching the kill floor machinery.

ELECTRA:
When my father gets back he's honour-bound
To kill you. He'll make a public show
Humiliate your stringy body –

FURY 2:
Don't rise to the bait, my love. The daughter's
Nasty: opportunity.

*FURY 2 jogs ELECTRA's arm, causing her to cut herself
and flinch. FURY 2 gets excited. AEGISTHUS: tries to
help her.*

ELECTRA:
Get off me! I'm fine.

AEGISTHUS:
                 You're not! It's deep.

ELECTRA looks at her finger and starts to faint.

ELECTRA:
Ugh! I can't!

AEGISTHUS:
                 Hold up your hand!
Press this on it.

*AEGISTHUS pulls out a handkerchief. ELECTRA sits down,
with her hand up. She's lost the initiative in the encounter.*

FURY 2:
Thirsty for blood . . .

AEGISTHUS:
                              Better?
Here, let me look.

FURY 2:
                              It's tempting.

He removes the handkerchief and licks the blood from the wound. ELECTRA snatches back her hand and tries to get away from him.

ELECTRA:
                                        What are you *doing*?

AEGISTHUS:
I didn't mean . . . I'm sorry.

ELECTRA:
                              You're *sick*!

FURY 2:
It was salty, such deep crimson
We couldn't resist it.

AEGISTHUS shakes his head, trying to ignore his FURY.

ELECTRA:
                    I've heard the rumours
About you and your disgusting father.

FURY 2:
Mm, the taste of Agamemnon's blood!

AEGISTHUS:
Watch what you say!

ELECTRA:
You don't tell me what to do.

AEGISTHUS:
There's a force behind language.
It never forgets. It burrows its way
Into your mind, like a spiders' eggs
Laid in the brain, a nest
Of ideas that crawl out at night . . .

FURY 2:
Ah, those delicate spider feet.
No part of the self that they can't reach!

ELECTRA:
You're ill.

AEGISTHUS:
       Oh no, I'm sane
But under more pressure than you. I hear
More voices.

ELECTRA:
          They should lock you up.

AEGISTHUS:
Don't you hear it? How words push
Where you don't want to go?

ELECTRA:
          I say
What I mean, mean what I say.

FURY 2:
                              Ah!
Touching. The innocence of youth!

ELECTRA:
I want you out of here, you creep.

AEGISTHUS:
Your mother knows. She hears it too.

*AEGISTHUS tries to go closer to ELECTRA, who backs off,
becoming entangled in the kill floor machinery.*

ELECTRA:
I think I know her better than you.

AEGISTHUS:
The ones before us. Knowing,
Not knowing.

FURY 2:
                    Find a weak spot,
Use her!

ELECTRA:
            I don't want to know.

AEGISTHUS:
Revulsion. Nausea in the nerves.

FURY 2:
Dead, want Agamemnon dead.

AEGISTHUS:
If I could vomit and be clean . . .

FURY 2:

Say it!

Do it! Agamemnon dead!

Under the influence of FURY 2 AEGISTHUS is starting a panic attack.

AEGISTHUS:
No! Not this again! Help me!

ELECTRA:
You don't fool me with that performance!

AEGISTHUS: (*losing control of his breath*)
Shit! . . . Don't want to listen!

ELECTRA:
That might have worked with . . . (*A beat's pause.*)
Are you all right?

AEGISTHUS:
She said you were gone . . . get . . . off my back . . .

ELECTRA:
I hate you but there's no need to take on . . .

He falls on his knees.

Hell! What? Are you having an attack
Or something?

*AEGISTHUS can't answer, and his hyperventilating increases.
ELECTRA makes to run out but can't leave him.*

What if he chokes?

ELECTRA, finally convinced, bends over him to check his airways are open, strokes his face to calm him down. Enter FURY 1 and CLYTEMNESTRA.

CLYTEMNESTRA:
What's happening here?

ELECTRA:
He had a funny turn, I thought
It was a trick at first but now . . .
I think he really *is* in trouble.

FURY 1:
He pulled that stunt before on you,
Now he wants Electra!

CLYTEMNESTRA:
No!
It's him and me against the world.

FURY 1:
Had mummy, now he wants the daughter.

CLYTEMNESTRA:
I thought I'd found a proper man
But I was wrong. Go back to that hole
I saved you from and rot alone.

AEGISTHUS:
Clytemnestra, don't throw me out . . .

FURY 2:
You'll have kill yourself . . .

AEGISTHUS: (*utterly debased*)
Please. Please.

FURY 2:
Or do what you know is right. Avenge!

CLYTEMNESTRA:
I took you in and this how you pay me.

AEGISTHUS:
Leave me alone! All of you!

FURY 2:
Now or never!

ELECTRA:
                    The man's beside
Himself. He's lost his mind.

AEGISTHUS: (*totally defeated by the FURY*)
                    Can't win . . .

CLYTEMNESTRA:
Since when did you speak up for him?

Fed by FURY 1.

Something's been happening.

ELECTRA:
                              It's in your head.
I know you've been under terrible strain
But this is crazy.

FURY 1:
                    I thought she did
Protest too much when he –

CLYTEMNESTRA:
I've been a fool. He has to go.

FURY 2:
Are you going to let a slip of a girl –

AEGISTHUS:
I want it to stop.

FURY 2:
                    I can make it go away.

AEGISTHUS:
Anything.

CLYTEMNESTRA:
How I despise a broken man!

FURY 2 speaks with AEGISTHUS, as if feeding him the words.

AEGISTHUS: (*shakily*)
Electra came on to me.
So I was kind –

ELECTRA:
                    What? He's lying.

AEGISTHUS:
Some women are very hard to refuse,
She kept on coming . . .

FURY 1:

Be fair, the girl is stubborn.

CLYTEMNESTRA:
I saw you.

ELECTRA:

You've got this wrong.

CLYTEMNESTRA:
Agamemnon should have sent for you
Instead of Iphigenia, they should have killed
You instead of her!

ELECTRA reacts as if slapped.

ELECTRA:
I don't know who you are anymore.

CLYTEMNESTRA:
Behave like a bitch in heat and you
Can run with the ferals.

ELECTRA:

You talk like a harridan,
Not my mother. I'd rather
Take my chance outside than stand by
And see all my father has dared to build
Ruined by people who aren't even fit
To serve at his table.

CLYTEMNESTRA:

You always were
Your father's daughter.

ELECTRA:

I honour my promises.

CLYTEMNESTRA advances on ELECTRA to dwarf her physically.

CLYTEMNESTRA:
So smug! And 'honour' has cost you what
Exactly? Oh, you've done your chores
Like a dutiful daughter but you're mediocre,
Conformist with no imagination
Or spark to see how things
Could be otherwise. No, the broken glass
Is left for people like me who are not afraid
To grasp the shards and not feel the cuts
Under the blood.

Turning to Aegisthus

And as for you,
You've slept with the mother, so now you prefer
The daughter?

AEGISTHUS:
No! No! Don't be silly!

CLYTEMNESTRA:
You must have been laughing. While my own
Were whispering, gossiping, making jokes . . .

AEGISTHUS:
I couldn't care less!

CLYTEMNESTRA:
                    I *have* to care.
I'm leader now but that could change
In a flash. They turn, I could be run
Out of the compound like a scabby dog
If the people decided –

AEGISTHUS: (*pushed by FURY 2 who is constantly whispering
                    in his ear*)
My father –

CLYTEMNESTRA: (*getting frantic*)
I can't believe I've risked everything
For you! Do you know what outside is like?
Ferals with nothing but what they can steal
From the likes of us. Have you heard how they treat
Women and children? You have to be in
A compound to live, don't you understand?

AEGISTHUS:
There is another way.

CLYTEMNESTRA:
Agamemnon will put me out. What was I thinking?
He'll be here any day now. I'll go
To meet him, explain you took advantage . . .

*The full physical union of FURY 2 and AEGISTHUS takes
place.*

AEGISTHUS:
I'll have to kill him.

Everyone holds still.

The FURIES make singing sounds, forcing the action through the rest of the scene.

                      Then would you
Trust me? It would be my gift to you.

ELECTRA:
Stop it! Tell him to stop it. Now!
He should never have come here.

FURY 2:
At long, long last, the boy's come good!
It took some work, but *this* will be worth it.

FURY 1:
Now we're talking!

AEGISTHUS:
He was wrong in so many ways. I'll take revenge
On your behalf. On my father's
And Iphigenia's. Show the world
They can't blot us out if we stand together.

ELECTRA:
This is insane. Call the men,
Get rid of him.

AEGISTHUS wipes his brow, his body language showing that he's not as confident as his words make out. AEGISTHUS gets more confident as he goes on.

AEGISTHUS:
Our families have treated us like shit
On their shoes. Who do they think they are?
Well, we can make alliances too.
Did they expect us just to roll over
And die of shame? Singly, we might
Have done that but now we're together.
Like the frost that topples the wall,
The flood that brings the ceiling down.
We'll avenge your daughter and my father
Make them remember us.

*AEGISTHUS and the FURIES circle CLYTEMNESTRA,
who's standing still, as if in a dream.*

ELECTRA:
It's not too late, this is only talk.
Throw him out, let's get back to normal.

CLYTEMNESTRA does nothing.

AEGISTHUS:
                              Can you sleep
With him again, knowing what he did?

CLYTEMNESTRA:
I can't. (*To ELECTRA*) Don't you see? Your father
Can never come back. His hands are dirty
With his own Iphigenia's blood.

ELECTRA:
So you'd murder him? That would be savage.

CLYTEMNESTRA:
I act as a mother! In self-defence.
He attacked my body, Iphigenia came out of me,
He treated her like a piece of meat.

ELECTRA:
He did the best for us.

CLYTEMNESTRA:
                        He's *used*
Me, Electra. If he cared
At all for his wife, he'd have fought
Free of the alliance, brought Iphigenia home
Safe to her mother.

AEGISTHUS:
                        He would.

CLYTEMNESTRA:
No one could blame me for taking the reins
Doing the right thing by my daughter.

AEGISTHUS:
It's true.

CLYTEMNESTRA:
            I wouldn't expect
A virgin to know about striking a blow
For mothers everywhere.

ELECTRA:
Clytemnestra, stop and think!
You need to wait and hear what happened,
Let Agamemnon have his say!

CLYTEMNESTRA: (*peak of the whipping up. She should be terrifying*)
I *will* not have any man say what I can do
I, Clytemnestra, act for myself.

Enter CHORUS 3, breathless.

CHORUS 3:
Fantastic news! We've seen the fires!
Agamemnon's on his way home.
He'll be here very shortly.

CLYTEMNESTRA:
No!

AEGISTHUS:
He'll kill me once Electra tells him.

ELECTRA goes to run out. AEGISTHUS drags her back.

CLYTEMNESTRA:
You'd go to your father? He's a butcher!
I'm begging you, let this run its course.

ELECTRA:
You shouldn't be doing this.

CLYTEMNESTRA:
                     But darling,
What father who deserves the name
Could kill his own daughter?

ELECTRA:

You don't know
What happened, so how can you decide
What's right and what's wrong in this situation?

AEGISTHUS:
He's nearly here. What shall we do with her?

CLYTEMNESTRA:
I've had enough of her whining on and on.
This one's no daughter of mine.
Do what you like but do it quickly.

Exit CLYTEMNESTRA.

AEGISTHUS:
Electra, dear. Do you have a temperature?
Dr Aegisthus feels he should
Do something fast to cool you down.

He kisses her and takes some layers of ELECTRA'S clothes off before closing her into the fridge, FURY 2 is ecstatic. ELECTRA bangs on the fridge desperate to get out, FURY 2 beats back on the fridge with horrible triumphalism.

SCENE 13

The kill floor. There are boxes all over the floor – Agamemnon's relief supplies. Enter CHORUS 3.

CHORUS 3: (*shouting to CHORUS 1 and 2 offstage*)
I told you they were here!

Enter CHORUS 1, and 2.

CHORUS 3:
                              I was sure
Agamemnon would come through!

CHORUS 1 falls to his knees.

CHORUS 2:
Come on, old thing, no need for that.
The sooner we get this stuff inside
The sooner we eat.

CHORUS 1: (*overcome*)
                              I thought we were dead
And done for. Human teeth look sharp
When hunger makes us animals
Again. But Agamemnon came!

CHORUS 3:
That label says tinned salmon! Ham!
There's a sack of new potatoes.

CHORUS 2:
Stop messing about, there's work to do!

CHORUS 3: (*gives CHORUS 1 a tissue*)
He's saved us, I didn't have to eat you!

CHORUS 2:
Those who help unload eat first!

CHORUS 3:
You'll get no argument from me!

*Enter AGAMEMNON. CASSANDRA hides behind the
machinery. CHORUS 3, 2 and 1 greet AGAMEMNON.*

AGAMEMNON:
I thought the last five miles would never end.
No welcoming committee?

CHORUS 1:
                Sir, no man
Was ever more welcome in his own home.

CHORUS 2:
Tell him what's happened, he needs to know!

AGAMEMNON:
Food first and speeches later, boys.
My face is itching. I need a shave
And a wash.

CHORUS 1:
        But before you do . . .

AGAMEMNON:
                I'm surprised
That Clytemnestra isn't here.

CHORUS 1:
She knows you've arrived. Things were very bad . . .

AGAMEMNON: *(gestures to the food boxes)*
That's what the war was all about
And now we see what we've achieved.

AGAMEMNON goes to a bucket in the corner of the room and washes his face.

                                        Oh! That's good!
Clean water! Sleeping in clothes
And body armour – all very well . . .
It will be good to rest at last
In a familiar bed. This place
Is clean enough.

CHORUS 1:
                    We've had no meat
For weeks, no use for the machines.

AGAMEMNON:
No wonder it's spotless.

CHORUS 2:
                        Did you see ferals?

CHORUS 3:
They were so close to the compound
We'd hear them at night.

AGAMEMNON:
                        Won't bother us again.
Strung like magpies on a farmer's fence!
Forget that now. Here's why I struggled home.

Enter CLYTEMNESTRA, who has changed into more formal dress. Enter AEGISTHUS and FURY 2 who watch the encounter.

CLYTEMNESTRA: (*all political smiles*)
We heard you were coming, but you made good speed,
You've surprised us a little. Please excuse
The mess.

AGAMEMNON:
                    Everything looks in very good order.

CLYTEMNESTRA:
I've done my best. Given that times have been hard,
The harvest poor. But, let me see you!
I hardly know you with that beard.

AGAMEMNON:
                                        Don't be so formal.

CLYTEMNESTRA:
I'm shy. How often does a conquering hero
One who's secured the compound's future,
Opened new trade routes, repulsed the ferals,
Dealt with the warlords, make his way home?

AGAMEMNON:
Don't overdo it.

CLYTEMNESTRA:
                    I hear you've got company,
A woman.

AGAMEMNON:
Not what you think. A Trojan girl,
Same age as –

CLYTEMNESTRA:
Iphigenia. Let's celebrate
Your triumph in a suitable way.

AGAMEMNON:
Later.

CLYTEMNESTRA:
Forgive me . . . It's been so long . . .

AGAMEMNON:
Leave us alone.

CHORUS leaves.

AGAMEMNON:
Clytemnestra. Underneath it's me, your husband.
You've lost a lot of weight.

He moves to touch her arm. She recoils and backs away from him.

CLYTEMNESTRA:
You're going too fast. I need time . . .

AGAMEMNON:
So where's Electra?

CLYTEMNESTRA:
She's not far. And very proud
Of her father.

AGAMEMNON:
>   Perhaps you'll let me prove
> It's me. Beneath the grime I smell
> The same.

CLYTEMNESTRA:
>   Let's put it to the test.

CLYTEMNESTRA leads him to the bedroom. Exeunt. Enter CASSANDRA at the kill floor entrance.

CASSANDRA:
> See that star? A knifepoint coming!
> So hot it leaves a trail of smoke!

The meld between AEGISTHUS and FURY 2 has become problematic, so they're like a badly tied couple in a three-legged race. AEGISTHUS keeps on trying to get away, but not with any conviction, he's physically extremely uncomfortable.

AEGISTHUS:
> Who's that?

FURY 2:
>   No one.

CASSANDRA:
>   My fellow victim!

AEGISTHUS:
> What did you say?

FURY 2:
> Clytemnestra's done her part,
> Now's the time. Kill Agamemnon.

CASSANDRA:
Poor Aegisthus! Always pushed around.
A father blurring into a brother,
Is that a sister or a mother?
Both, both! No wonder you want
To act the son.

AEGISTHUS:
My father wants –

CASSANDRA:
                    Don't listen to that.
They use us to kill then, after the murder
Throw us away while we still live.

FURY 2 pushes her away from him and kicks her. She ends up against the fridge.

FURY 2:
Shut up!

CASSANDRA:
                    You're right to resist him!
That's the measure of a man –
How hard he fights against the pressures!
For once don't let them push you around.
I hear them screaming too and refuse
The part they push me to. So can you!

Despite FURY 2's best efforts, AEGISTHUS is compelled by CASSANDRA who reaches out to touch him. He recoils, but nurses the touch, as if wounded. Enter CLYTEMNESTRA.

CLYTEMNESTRA:
Where's the knife?

AEGISTHUS: (*hyperventilating*)
                    I had a part
But I've forgotten . . . Had a story
But it's let me down. Think!

CLYTEMNESTRA:
He's ready and waiting! Doesn't suspect
A thing.

AEGISTHUS:
            No . . .This way . . .
Some peace of mind, at least. If not . . .

FURY 2:
I'll tear you to pieces.

AEGISTHUS:
                    So tired, so tired
Of being bullied . . .

CLYTEMNESTRA:
                    Aegisthus
Don't let me down. You promised me this . . .

AEGISTHUS:
She touched me! Everything
Goes through her like smoke!

CLYTEMNESTRA:
                            Aegisthus!

AEGISTHUS:
So tired . . . (*Screams*) Now I see you,
Get off me, you're hardly human. I
Refuse.

FURY 2:
>This one's useless.
I warned you. Now go out of your mind.

FURY 2 begins to leave AEGISTHUS'S body and tosses him aside in disgust. This causes him great pain, he's a broken person. FURY 1 takes the knife from him and, with great ceremony, presents it to CLYTEMNESTRA.

CLYTEMNESTRA:
Damn you. I delivered. (*Pause*). What?
You want me to . . .?

FURY 1: (*very softy and eerily*)
>The hand knows what to do.
No need for rehearsal.

CLYTEMNESTRA:
>But I'm his wife.
That wasn't the deal. I'm already so far
Out on a limb they could kill me
For talking to him . . .

FURY 1:
>Things have changed.
Who better to do it? Don't pretend
You haven't imagined how it would feel
To kill him yourself!

CLYTEMNESTRA:
>I want what's right
But I'm no executioner.

FURY 1:
Your daughter's blood speaks loud and clear.
This is the way to honour her.
To wash the body, fold her arms
Over her bruised and bitten chest . . .

CLYTEMNESTRA:
I was never allowed to brush her hair
Before . . .

FURY 1:
                    Do it now! Don't think!

CLYTEMNESTRA:
The only veins cut open can't
Be hers . . . But I'm not strong enough
To kill a soldier . . .

FURY 1:
                              Iphigenia's veins
Demand another body! It's two
Against one. I'll give you all the strength
You need but, Clytemnestra, do it now!

CLYTEMNESTRA:
Another weight to balance how
She fell! Murderers become
Dead meat! A second and it's done,
A blow for mothers and their children.

*Exeunt CLYTEMNESTRA and FURY 1 to bedroom. Lights
up on ELECTRA, who starts beating at the walls of the fridge.
CASSANDRA emerges from her hiding place and lets
ELECTRA out of the fridge.*

CASSANDRA:
The blood choir's singing now! I'm foam,
This family's a wave that's breaking.
They'll come for you.
The Furies always drive you mad
They make it seem so plausible.
Promise me you won't be fooled.
And then they kill you by another's hand.

ELECTRA:
What's happening?

CASSANDRA:
A daughter like me, you have a choice.

ELECTRA:
Help me.

CASSANDRA:
       I did. It's time.

Exit CASSANDRA.

SCENE 14

CLYTEMNESTRA'S bedroom. She's bloody next to Agamemnon's dead body

CLYTEMNESTRA:
This is the high that soldiers feel
After the skirmish! What it's like to act
With might and right! Now I'm blooded . . .
I didn't bear a child to have
Her killed. I've found the sweet spot
In my mind: a mother's revenge.

Enter CASSANDRA.

Come in, my girl. Behold your hero.

CASSANDRA:
Oh you weak and foolish woman.

CLYTEMNESTRA:
Weak? I've only started being strong!

CASSANDRA:
I heard them too! You've given in
To Furies, they're phantoms,
Not fully real.

CLYTEMNESTRA:
                    No, I've executed
A murderer.

CASSANDRA:
                    He was a good man.

CLYTEMNESTRA:
Not to me. Or Iphigenia.

CASSANDRA:
You've killed yourself as surely as if that blood
Were yours and passed the madness to your children.

CASSANDRA goes to the door and shouts.

Roses bloom and it's a blood bouquet
For Electra! Clytemnestra murders
Her own children!

CLYTEMNESTRA jumps on CASSANDRA.

CLYTEMNESTRA:
          This is sweet:
A baby rabbit squeaking to nasty
Hawk above her. She's telling lies!

CASSANDRA: (*her voice getting louder and more confident*)
I'm perfectly safe. It's only a part.
I'll stand again in just a minute.
They're going to turn aside, their eyes
Will follow others through the dark
And you won't be you any more.

*CLYTEMNESTRA kills CASSANDRA. Enter CHORUS 1, 3
and ELECTRA and FURY 2. ELECTRA screams. This is the
sound of the new reality and it makes everybody understand
what's happened.*

CLYTEMNESTRA:
I was born to do this . . . Once you let go
It's surprising the force you find in yourself . . .

They drove me to it! Feel how lush
And fertile . . .

ELECTRA:

        Oh, my father!

CHORUS 2:
No feral could do worse than this,
It's savage.

ELECTRA wails.

*CLYTEMNESTRA is on a high, she hasn't noticed that FURY
1 has disengaged from her and is turning her attentions to
ELECTRA. As FURY 1 leaves, CLYTEMNESTRA's
assurance collapses in front of us. Throughout this scene,
ELECTRA becomes physically and vocally larger, and
CLYTEMNESTRA is diminished as the FURY leaves her.*

*FURIES 1 and 2 approach ELECTRA as they did
CLYTEMNESTRA and CASSANDRA at the beginning
of the play. Reprise of same musical theme.*

CLYTEMNESTRA:
Tell me how good I was! I shone!

ELECTRA:
What on earth possessed you?

CLYTEMNESTRA: (*trying to get the FURY 1's attention*)
I acted . . . did it with style . . .
Say something!

ELECTRA:

        What's that humming?

CLYTEMNESTRA sees that the FURIES have gone to ELECTRA, who now dominates the stage with CLYTEMNESTRA at her feet.

CLYTEMNESTRA:
Remember, Electra, I'm your mother.

END

Sherman Cymru Publications:
Maes Terfyn (Gwyneth Glyn)
The Almond and the Seahorse
(Kaite O'Reilly)
Yr Argae (Conor McPherson –
cyf. Cymraeg Wil Sam Jones)
Amgen : Broken (Gary Owen)
Ceisio'i Bywyd Hi (Martin Crimp –
cyf. Cymraeg Owen Martell)
Cardboard Dad (Alan Harris)
Llwyth (Dafydd James)
Cityscape (Emily Steel, Tracy Harris,
Bethan Marlow, Kit Lambert)
Gadael yr Ugeinfed Ganrif
(Gareth Potter)
Cinders & Plum (...and me, Will!)
(Louise Osborn)
Desire Lines (Ian Rowlands)
Sgint (Bethan Marlow)

Dalier Sylw Publications:
Y Cinio (Geraint Lewis)
Hunllef yng Nghymru Fydd
(Gareth Miles)
Epa yn y Parlwr Cefn (Siôn Eirian)
Wyneb yn Wyneb (Meic Povey)
"i" (Jim Cartwright –
cyf. Cymraeg John Owen)
Fel Anifail (Meic Povey)
Croeso Nôl (Tony Marchant –
cyf. Cymraeg John Owen)
Bonansa! (Meic Povey)
Tair (Meic Povey).

Sgript Cymru Publications:
Diwedd y Byd/Yr Hen Blant (Meic
Povey)
Art and Guff (Catherine Treganna)
Crazy Gary's Mobile Disco (Gary
Owen)
Ysbryd Beca (Geraint Lewis)
Franco's Bastard (Dic Edwards)
Dosbarth (Geraint Lewis)
past away (Tracy Harris)
Indian Country (Meic Povey)
Diwrnod Dwynwen (Fflur Dafydd,
Angharad Devonald, Angharad Elen,
Meleri Wyn James, Dafydd Llywelyn,
Nia Wyn Roberts)
Ghost City (Gary Owen)
AMDANI! (Bethan Gwanas)
Community Writer 2001-2004
(Robert Evans, Michael Waters et al)
Drws Arall i'r Coed (Gwyneth Glyn,
Eurgàin Haf, Dyfrig Jones, Caryl
Lewis, Manon Wyn)
Crossings (Clare Duffy)
Life of Ryan... and Ronnie
(Meic Povey)
Cymru Fach (Wiliam Owen Roberts)
Orange (Alan Harris)
Hen Bobl Mewn Ceir (Meic Povey)
Aqua Nero (Meredydd Barker)
Buzz (Meredydd Barker)

Available from:
Sherman Cymru
Senghennydd Road,
Cardiff, CF24 4YE
029 2064 6900

Range of titles also available from:
amazon.co.uk/shops/sherman_cymru
http://www.shermancymru.co.uk/
playtext/